Twenties:
Finding Your Way

ABHILASHA BAFNA

BookLeaf Publishing
India | USA | UK

Presentation by *BookLeaf Publishing*

Web: www.bookleafpub.com

E-mail: info@bookleafpub.com

ISBN: 9789363302464

First edition 2024

To the dreamers, the lost, and the hopeful. To those who question the path ahead and yearn for something more. May this book be a companion on your journey, offering solace, inspiration, and the courage to embrace your true self.

To my incredible family and friends, whose unwavering support has been my constant source of strength. And to all those who seek to find their way, may this book be a guiding light.

To the wonderful community of readers who embraced 'Let's Talk Life,' thank you for being a part of this shared experience. Your insights and conversations have enriched my understanding of the human condition and made me feel connected to a wider world.

Your connection with 'Let's Talk Life' fueled my passion for writing and gave me the courage to delve deeper into the challenges and triumphs of life. Your support has been invaluable in shaping my journey as an author.

For more content, updates, and to connect
with the author, scan the following QR codes to
visit her Instagram and Quora profiles.

Instagram:

Quora:

ACKNOWLEDGEMENT

I would like to express my sincere gratitude to the countless individuals whose experiences and insights have shaped this book. Your stories, shared openly and honestly, have been the heart and soul of this project. To the friends, family, and mentors who have supported and encouraged me throughout this journey, thank you for your unwavering belief in my vision. A special thanks to those who shared their personal stories with such vulnerability. Your courage has inspired countless others.

I am also grateful to the countless individuals who have contributed to the world of personal development and self-help. Your work has been a source of inspiration and guidance.

Drawing from the lessons learned in 'Let's Talk Life,' I sought to offer guidance and support to those navigating the complex landscape of their twenties.

The overwhelming response to 'Let's Talk Life' inspired me to delve deeper into the challenges and joys of personal growth, leading to the creation of 'Twenties- Finding Your Way.

Finally, I would like to thank my readers for choosing to embark on this journey with me. Your support and feedback are invaluable.

PREFACE

Your twenties are a whirlwind. A decade of self-discovery, heartbreaks, triumphs, and endless possibilities. It's a time when you're expected to have it all figured out, yet you feel more lost than ever. This book is an honest reflection of that journey. It's a collection of stories, insights, and advice from those who've walked this path before you. It's a reminder that it's okay to feel uncertain, to make mistakes, and to redefine yourself along the way. Let's navigate this decade together.

INDEX

Early Twenties: Exploration and Growth

1. **Stuck in a Loop** - Initial confusion or feeling stuck.

2. **Left Behind** - Comparing oneself to peers or feeling left out.

3. **New Path** - A sense of new beginnings or a change in direction.

4. **Childhood Sweethearts** - Reflecting on past relationships or childhood experiences.

5. **Tough Times** - Addressing challenges or difficulties.

6. **Twenties Twirl** - A playful exploration of the twenties.

7. **Feeling Lost** - Experiencing uncertainty or confusion.

8. **A Woman's World** - Exploring gender roles or personal identity.

9. **Love's Sweet Lesson** - Learning about love and relationships.

10. **From Theory to Reality** - Transitioning from ideas to actions.

11. **Why's Life So Tough?**

12. **Social Media Shuffle**

13. **Lost in the Maze**

Mid-Twenties: Reflection and Maturity

14. **A Lifetime of Inspiration: Sibling, The Elder** - Learning from a sibling or mentor.

15. **Watching You Grow, the younger one!** - Nurturing or mentoring someone younger.

16. **From Rebel to Respect: A Tribute to parents** - Personal growth and maturity, understanding parents.

17. **Shine on Mom**

18. **Twenties: A Time of Finding Our Way** - A general theme of self-discovery.

19. **"Growing Up with Birthdays"** - Reflecting on aging or milestones.

20. **"What is Love?"** - Exploring the nature of love or relationships.

21. **Anger: A Double-Edged Sword -** Managing emotions, particularly anger.

22. **"Emotional Rollercoaster: Mid-Twenties"** - Experiencing ups and downs.

23. **Mistakes? No Way!**

24. **Gratitude > Insecurity**

25. **Narcissist Women**

26. **Narcissist Men**

27. **Silent Tears**

28. **The Shine Faded**

29. **Overplanning Underdoing**

30. **Lost and Found**

31. **Beyond the Reflection**

32. **Karma's Cycle: Breakdowns and Comebacks** - Overcoming challenges and resilience.

33. **Life's Canvas**

Late Twenties: Connection and Purpose

34. **Communication: The Key to Connection** - Importance of communication in relationships.

35. **The Rat Race of Twenties** - Societal pressures or career struggles.

36. **Beyond the Office Walls**

37. **Life's Three Stages: Childhood, Teenage and Adulthood** - Reflecting on life stages.

38. **Gender Roles: A Changing Landscape** - Exploring evolving gender roles.

39. **A Man's Heart** - Perspectives from a masculine viewpoint.

40. **A Woman's Heart** - Perspectives from a feminine viewpoint.

41. **Love's Compass**

42. **Food, Friends, and Fitness**

43. **Millennials, Gen Z, and Alphas: A Comparison** - Comparing generations.

44. **Finding Your Calling - Paths to Passion** - Discovering purpose or career paths.

45. **Unheard Apologies** - Unresolved conflicts or regrets.

46. **Daughter's Delight** - Celebrating family relationships.

47. **A Debt-ridden Dream** - Financial challenges or aspirations.

48. **The Human Puzzle - Karma's Cosmic Game** - Philosophical reflections on life.

49. **A Different Perspective** - Seeing things from a new angle.

50. **The Power of Words** - The impact of language and communication.

51. **Healing Through Art** - Exploring creativity as a form of therapy.

52. **The Pressure to Settle Down** - Societal expectations and personal desires.

53. **You Are Number One**

54. **Reconnection**

55. **Calling My Soul Home**

Early Twenties:
Exploration and Growth

Stuck in a Loop

Scared to try, scared to fall,
Stuck in a corner, building a wall.
Fears got a grip, it won't let go,
Just sitting around, feeling low.

Blaming others, a wasted art,
Losing myself, a broken heart.
Where's the purpose, where's the why?
Just questions floating, up in the sky.

I know it's scary, to step outside,
But staying in here, is no place to hide.
Facing the fear, it's the only way,
To build a new me, come what may.

Left Behind

All gone ahead, left behind,
Feeling lonely, losing my mind.
Trying to catch up, it's no fun,
Everyone's racing, like someone won.
Used to be friends, now strangers, it's true,
Where did they go?
What should I do?
Lost in the crowd, feeling small,
Wish I could shout, and tell them all.

But my voice is quiet, a whisper in the air,
No one to hear me, no one to care.
Stuck in this moment, a lonely place,
Searching for answers, finding no trace.

New Path

A light's come on, a brighter day,
Found a purpose, in a special way.
Excited, nervous, a mix of both,
Walking a new path, a hopeful oath.

Don't know the steps, or where it leads,
But I'm ready to face, whatever it needs.
No more giving up, no looking back,
Just moving forward, on the right track.

Still a bit lost, unsure where to go,
But I'll figure it out, that's all I know.
With every step, a little more clear,
This new journey, I'll hold so dear.

Childhood Sweethearts

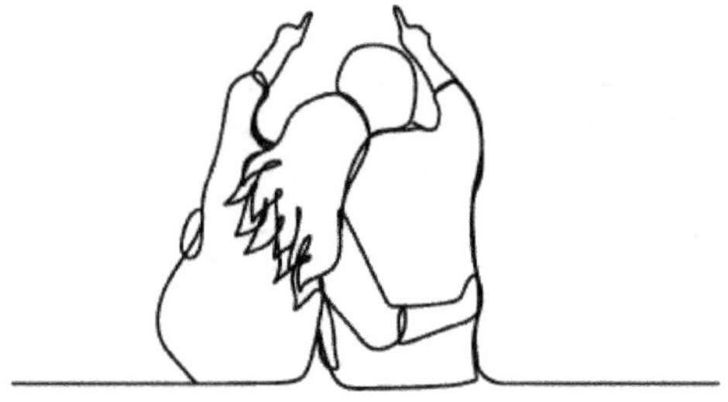

We grew up together, side by side,
Best friends forever, our special guide.
Shared secrets, dreams, and laughter bright,
Through sunshine and storms, we've seen the
light.

We know each other, through and through,
A loyal partner, me and you.
Side by side, we'll face the years,
Together we'll conquer all our fears.

We've helped each other, stood strong and true,
A bond so special, me and you.
More than lovers, a trusted friend,
Our story together, knows no end.

Tough Times

Life was sweet, a happy tune,
Then came the storm, a dark afternoon.
Money troubles, a heavy load,
Working hard, on life's rough road.

We climbed the ladder, almost there,
But fate was tricky, a sudden scare.
Lost it all, felt like a game,
Heartbroken, lost in life's crazy fame.

Days were tough, nights were long,
But love was strong, a powerful song.
Hand in hand, we faced the fight,
Determined to rise, with all our might.

Like phoenixes, we'll soar and shine,
Stronger than ever, a brand-new line.
With hearts aflame, we'll face the test,
And build a future, truly blessed.

Twenties Twirl

Twenties, a whirlwind, fast and bright,
Relationships fading, out of sight.
Friendships once strong, now feeling thin,
Promises broken, where do we begin?

A lifetime together, that's what it seemed,
Now just a memory, a distant dream.
Siblings drifting, partners apart,
Lost in the shuffle, a heavy heart.

Work and life, a constant chase,
Missing moments, at a frantic pace.
Formal hellos, a hollow sound,
Once close connections, nowhere to be found.

A puzzle to solve, a tricky art,
Balancing it all, a heavy heart.
But through the chaos, we'll find our way,
To cherish the moments, come what may.

Feeling Lost

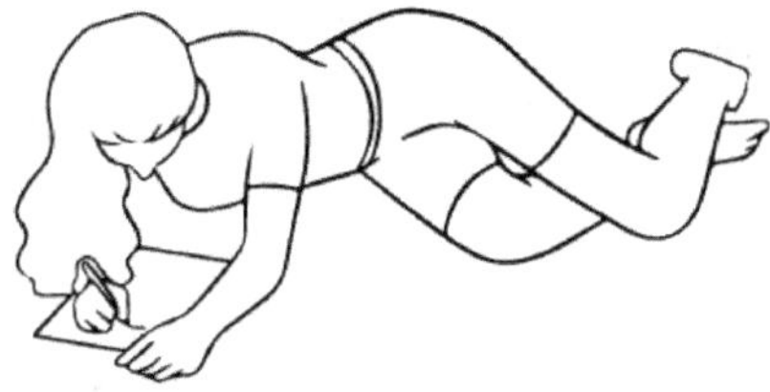

Feeling stuck, like a record on repeat,
No clear direction, no place to retreat.
The world's a blur, colors gone gray,
Lost in the shadows, come what may.

Family, friends, love, once a shield,
Now feel like weights, a heavy field.
Broken inside, pieces scattered around,
Every connection, a hollow sound.

Comparing lives, an endless race,
Feeling behind, a losing chase.
Claws and teeth, a constant fight,
People around, a blinding light.

Work feels distant, a foggy dream,
Mind wandering, a lost-at-sea scene.
Despair knocking, a haunting fear,
How to carry on, year after year.

Just want to hide, disappear from sight,
Escape this darkness, find the light.
One step at a time, that's all I can do,
Hoping for better, something new.

A Woman's World

In twenties, a world unfolds,
Dreams woven, stories untold.
She builds her career, a steady climb,
Balancing work, life, a delicate rhyme.

Late nights, deadlines, a constant race,
Yet she finds solace, a peaceful space.
With friends, she laughs, worries fade,
Alone, she walks, her spirit unafraid.

Dresses she wears, a fashion's hue,
But gazes follow, a judgment new.
Traditionals adorn, a cultural grace,
Yet eyes still linger, a haunting chase.

Is it the clothes, or minds that roam?
Unsafe she feels, a stranger in her home.
In what outfit, where to be free?
A woman's safety, a mystery.

To break the chains, a courage bold,
Challenge the norms, stories untold.
For safety lies not in attire or place,
But in minds that change, embrace.

Love's Sweet Lesson

Love, a feeling pure and deep,
A teacher wise, a friend to keep.
It shows us truths, no other can,
A raw, exposed, vulnerable man.

Sometimes sweet, sometimes a test,
Love's lessons learned, the very best.
Even when it fades, a gift it leaves,
A life-changing lesson, it believes.

If it stays, a diamond you'll become,
Pure and true, a heart that's sum.
Love's magic touch, a guiding light,
A precious jewel, shining bright.

From Theory to Reality

Twenty years old, a fresh start,
Learning and working, a clever art.
Internships, lessons outside the school,
Life's realities, a helpful tool.

Tough at first, but I found my way,
Into the flow, day by day.
Theoretical life, so far away,
Practical world, a brighter day.

Books taught me much, but life's a game,
Choices, needs, a burning flame.
More I wanted, more I sought to learn,
People's nature, a constant churn.

Some good, some tricky, sly, and smart,
Real or fake, a playing part.
Everyone's struggles, unique and deep,
A decade of discovery, a journey to keep.

Why's Life So Tough?

Life's a tricky game, it's true,
Keeps throwing curveballs, at me and you.
It pushes, shoves, a mean old tease,
But guess what? You're still at ease!

'Cause every challenge, every fight,
Makes you stronger, shining bright.
Like a muscle, you'll get tough,
Overcome the rough, that's enough!

So lift your head, and smile so wide,
You'll conquer life's crazy tide.
You're awesome, that's the deal,
Life's just a test, you'll always heal.

Social Media Shuffle

Scroll, like, share, repeat the game,
A digital world, a crazy fame.
Filters and stories, a colorful show,
Connections formed, where friendships grow.

But hey, don't let it steal your shine,
Real life's magic, truly divine.
Balance is key, a perfect blend,
Online and offline, world without end.

So let's connect, but stay grounded too,
Real smiles and hugs, something truly new.
Let's spread kindness, like seeds we sow,
In this digital garden, let love grow!

Lost in the Maze

A path unclear, a heart unsure,
Dreams and doubts, a constant blur.
Will I find my place, my shining light,
Or fade into shadows, lost from sight?

Each day a battle, to push or to yield,
Fear of failure, a painful shield.
Time ticks on, and hope starts to wane,
But courage whispers, "Try once again."

The answer lies not in haste or delay,
But steady steps, day by day.
Believe in yourself, let your spirit soar,
Your dream awaits, just open the door.

MID-TWENTIES:
Reflection and Maturity

A Lifetime of Inspiration: Sibling, The Elder one

Hey elder brother, how's it going?
I've never told you, but it's true.
You've been my rock, my guiding star,
Since I was little, from near and far.

You've inspired me, made me feel so cool,
Working so hard, following your rule.
Independent woman, I've become,
Thanks to you, my guiding sum.

A father figure, not always right,
But always there, shining your light.
You've given us more, than what you had,
A life of comfort, so glad.

**I'm so grateful, for your love and care,
My mentor, my guide, always there.**

From childhood days, to adulthood's grace,
Your love and support, a warm embrace.
You've taught me strength, resilience, and pride,
A beacon of hope, my guiding tide.

**Through thick and thin, you've always been
there,**

**A constant support, beyond compare.
Your selfless acts, your kindest heart,
A treasure I'll forever guard.**

Thank you for everything, my dear elder
brother,
A bond unbreakable, forever together.
Your love and guidance, a precious gift,
A legacy of kindness, a heart that's swift.

Watching You Grow, the younger one!

Hey little bro, my heart's delight,
A bundle of joy, shining bright.
From childhood days, to adulthood's grace,
Your love and support, a warm embrace.

A protector, a friend, a guiding star,
Always there, no matter how near or far.
Through thick and thin, you've stood by me,
A constant source of strength, wild and free.

Fighting for me, when no one else would,
A loyal brother, brave and good.
Respecting my work, my dreams, my goals,
A supportive friend, who always consoles.

From asking for pocket money, to earning his
own,
You've grown so much, a man of your own.
Struggling to build your career, with passion and
drive,
A future so bright, you'll surely thrive.

Our bond is unbreakable, a love so deep,
A treasure I'll forever keep.
A little brother, a precious gem,
A love that's pure, like heaven's stem.

From Rebel to Respect: From Rebel to Respect: A Tribute to Parents

Twenty, a decade of growth,
From college days, to life's rough coast.
A grown adult, earning my keep,
Struggling with bills, so deep.

Once a rebel, against their will,
Ignoring **parents'** advice, with a stubborn thrill.
But now I see, **parents'** wisdom's true,
Their experiences, guiding me through.

In the end, I've become like them,
Understanding **parents'** love, a precious gem.
Their opinions, for my benefit,
Caring not for the world, **their** heartfelt wit.

How ironic, it took a decade to see,
Their love and wisdom, meant for me.
Their understanding, a treasure so rare,
A love that's always been there.

From childhood days, to adulthood's grace,
Parents' love and support, a warm embrace.
A journey of growth, a transformation's art,
A twenty-something's heart.

Now I see the truth in all you said,
The wisdom in your words, ahead.
Once I argued, with a stubborn pride,
But now I understand, and can't hide
My gratitude for all you've done,
The love you've shown, beneath the sun.

A journey of growth, a lesson learned,
Their love and support, forever earned.
For guiding me through, with steadfast grace,
I offer my thanks, a warm embrace.

Parents are the best support one can have,
A love that's constant, unwavering and brave.

Shine on Mom

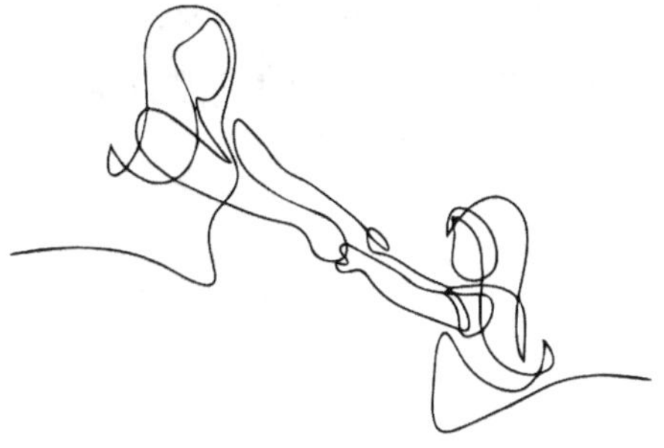

Mom, the strongest in the house, you see,
Holds it all together, just wait and agree.
She yells sometimes, it might sting a bit,
But mostly 'cause we're sad or doing things not
quite right.

She worries a lot, wants to keep us all safe,
Like a mama bear, from danger's chafe.
The world's a tricky place, that much is true,
Her protectiveness, a love shining through.

She might get mad, but it fades real quick,
'Cause seeing us happy makes her heart tick.
No controlling ways, just watchful care,
Guiding our steps, a burden to share.

Respect her always, show all moms you meet,
Love like theirs is oh so sweet.
One day they might not be here to fuss,
So cherish them now, 'cause love's a must.

Twenties: A Time of Finding Our Way

In twenties, life's a puzzle, a mystery to solve,
We search for our purpose, our passion to
evolve.
From one job to another, we try and explore,
To find what we're meant for, what we're here for.

A dream house, a car, a foreign trip,
But more than possessions, a soul to equip.
We want to make a difference, leave our mark,
To find our true calling, no matter how dark.

We face challenges, doubts, and fears,
But with resilience, we dry our tears.
We learn from mistakes, we rise and fall,
But through it all, we find our call.

In twenties, we're young, we're free,
To shape our lives, to be all we can be.

Growing Up with Birthdays

In childhood, birthdays were a sweet delight,
Distributing chocolates, a joyful sight.
After dinner, stories told with glee,
A family's bond, wild and free.

In college days, parties were a blast,
With friends around, time flew so fast.
Laughter, music, and dancing galore,
Memories to cherish, forevermore.

In mid-twenties, a change of pace,
A quiet celebration, a peaceful space.
Craving solitude, a moment's rest,
To reflect on life, put to the test.

From youthful glee to thoughtful grace,
Birthdays mark our journey's pace.
A time to celebrate, to reflect, to grow,
As life's chapters unfold, we come to know.

What is Love?

I'm a feeling that's warm and bright,
A connection that's pure and right.
I'm a dance, a song, a sweet delight.
I'm a journey, a wonderful sight.

I can make you laugh,
I can make you cry,
I can fill your heart, I can make you fly.
I'm a mystery, a puzzle, a surprise.
I'm a gift from heaven, a beautiful prize.

What am I?

... Love, of course!

Anger: A Double-Edged Sword

A tempest rages, a fiery storm,
A heart aflame, a spirit torn.
Rage consumes, a blinding heat,
A mind consumed, a bitter defeat.

Pros:
A burst of energy, a fiery might,
A surge of power, a righteous fight.
A voice that's heard, a stand that's taken,
A problem solved, a wrong forsaken.

Cons:
A blinding rage, a clouded mind,
A hurtful tongue, a heart unkind.
A broken bond, a lost friend,
A reputation tarnished, to the very end.

So, choose your path, with wisdom's guide,
Let anger serve, with righteous pride.
But temper it well, with reason's art,
And let it fuel, a noble heart.

Emotional Rollercoaster: Mid-Twenties

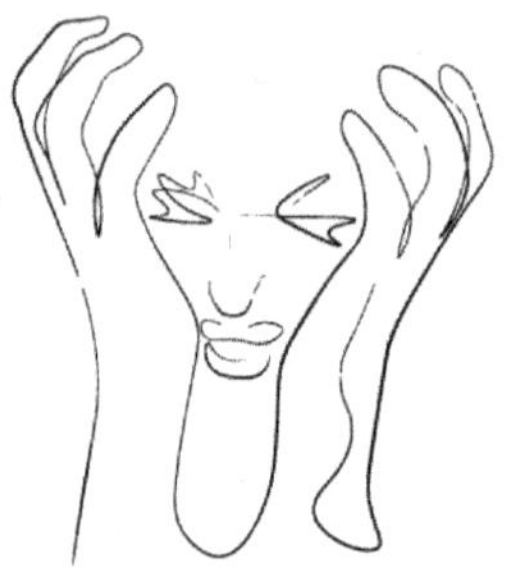

A whirlwind of change, a rollercoaster ride,
Mid-twenties, a time to confide.
Emotions run deep, a complex maze,
A tapestry woven, in countless ways.

Ambition and dreams, a burning fire,
Fear and doubt, a heavy desire.
Love and loss, a bittersweet blend,
Happiness and sadness, a never-ending trend.

Uncertainty lingers, a constant guest,
As life's path unfolds, a challenging test.
Self-discovery blooms, a journey of growth,
Finding one's purpose, a heartfelt oath.

So let emotions flow, a natural tide,
Embrace the journey, with open stride.
Mid-twenties, a time to explore,
To find oneself, forevermore.

Mistakes? No Way!

Everyone makes oops, it's true,
Learning lessons, something new.
So don't sweat it, don't be blue,
Mistakes are friends, let's see it through.

Plan it out, think it through,
Double-check, that's what you do.
Learn from others, wise and cool,
Mistakes? Not for a superstar like you!

So take a chance, don't be afraid,
Mistakes are stepping stones, well-made.
You'll grow and shine, a bright parade,
Mistakes? Just a tiny, silly shade!

Gratitude > Insecurity

Insecurity can definitely be destructive.
It can chip away at our self-esteem,
hold us back from trying new things,
and damage our relationships.

Gratitude, on the other hand, is a builder.
It helps us appreciate the good things in our
lives, both big and small.
This can boost our confidence, make us more
resilient,
and open us up to new possibilities.

By focusing on gratitude,
we can slowly but surely crowd out those
negative thoughts and insecurities. It's not a
one-time fix,
but it's a powerful tool to have in your mental
toolbox.

Narcissist Women

Her confidence, a blowin' horn,
But deep inside, she feels forlorn.
Bossy words and selfish ways,
Can't stand to see another's praise.

Green with envy, eyes burnin' bright,
Success of others, just ain't right.
Puts down your wins, with a nasty smirk,
Only her reflection, deserves a perk.
No room for kindness, just her own gain,
A one-way street, in pouring rain.
See her for what she truly is,
A tangled mess, with hidden fizz.

She never admits a single flaw,
It's always you, with the crooked straw.
Mistakes are yours, the blame you share,
Her perfect world, a burden to bear.

You don't deserve that drama show,
Walk away, let your good heart grow.
True love's gentle, warm and bright,
Not a storm cloud, dimming your light.

Leave her to her lonely throne,
You'll rise above, and claim your own.

Narcissist Men

His charm's a flash, his words a boast,
But deep down, insecurities are utmost.
He struts and brags, a know-it-all,
Never wrong, he'll stand ten feet tall.
Blames you for his mistakes, you see,
His perfect world, a fantasy.

He thinks you'll wait, come crawling back,
No matter the hurt, the nasty crack.
A king in his mind, though lonely and cold,
A tangled web of stories untold.

Jealousy simmers, a burning pyre,
When others shine, his anger fuels the fire.
He puts them down, to feel more grand,
But his empty heart, won't understand.

Don't get caught up in his twisted game,
This one-sided love, a burning shame.
Walk away free, with head held high,
From someone's love that's all a lie.

True love respects, it doesn't break,
It lifts you up, for goodness sake.
Leave him to his self-made maze,
You'll find your path, in brighter days.

Silent Tears

In your own home, a shadow falls,
A silent tension fills the walls.
Your smile once bright, now dimmed with pain,
Disrespectful words, a constant refrain.

You hold it in, for love and peace,
But worry lines show your heart's release.
Why should you bear this heavy weight,
In a place meant for love, not filled with hate?

We see your strength, your gentle grace,
And tears we'll wipe from your worried face.
Your voice deserves to rise and say,
"This disrespect will not hold sway."

We'll stand beside you, hand in hand,
A daughter's love, a loyal band.
For in this home, respect shall bloom,
And chase away the gathering gloom.

The Shine Faded

Life was sweet, work and play, a perfect mix.
Friends and family, the bestest clicks.
I climbed the ladder, feeling so alive,
But then things changed, like a bad movie vibe.

People got weird, copying what I do,
Jealous looks, instead of cheering, boo-hoo.
Likes and shares, a constant game,
My own life felt like a crazy shame.

I worked so hard, for my dreams to come true,
But now it feels like, "What am I gonna do?"
The people I loved, turned into a fight,
Lost in the crowd, feeling outta sight.

Overplanning, Underdoing

Planning too much and doing nothing is a phase
I am into.
I plan everyday, the things I want and what I
want to become.
However, I failed to focus on my current tasks,
Forgetting, "one thing at a time" was the rule.

And this is when I found,
How and where my goals were being disrupted,
How my passion into it became just a thing to
be achieved for the fame.
A vision lost in the noise,
a dream fading in the game.
It's time to break free, from this endless maze,
To find my true path, in simpler days.

Lost and Found

Caught in a whirlwind of wanting more,
Chasing dreams, but feeling sore.
Tired of running, always behind,
Losing myself, leaving friends behind.

Stuck in a box, trying to fit in,
Hiding my true self, a heavy sin.
It's time to break free, to be me,
Find my own path, wild and free.

Let's stop comparing, let's start living,
Building a life where joy is giving.
It's not about titles or fame,
But finding peace, a different game.

So let go of the stress, the endless chase,
Embrace your uniqueness, find your place.
You're special, one of a kind,
A beautiful soul, with a brilliant mind.

Beyond the Reflection

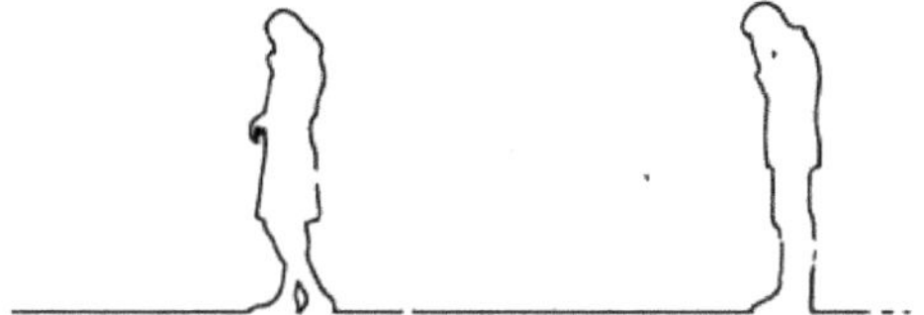

Started neck and neck, pushing each other on,
Wins felt like sunshine, losses dragged on.
Thought we were tight, but something was
wrong, you see,
My wins met with silence, a puzzling decree.

Style started shifting, a copycat's trend,
My choices reflected, a borrowed extend.
Made a funny clip, meant for lighthearted cheer,
But doubt whispered worries, a growing fear.

Hit "send," then a pause, a finger on undo,
Knowing laughter wouldn't bloom, just
suspicion anew.
Real connections lift you, that's the key, you see,
Not a constant battle, a race where no one can
agree.

So I'm walking away, from this one-sided show,
Looking for circles where good vibes can flow.
Because real connections, with laughter and grace,
Bloom where spirits can soar, not in a mirrored chase.

Karma's Cycle: Breakdowns and Comebacks

Mid-twenties, a storm's fierce bite,
Breakdowns strike, a chilling plight.
Alone or with support, we fall,
But rise again, heeding the call.

Uncharted paths, a journey unknown,
Yet we move on, a spirit unshown.
Good deeds sow seeds, a harvest of grace,
Bad deeds reap storms, a bitter taste.

Karma's game, a cosmic test,
A calculation, put to the best.
From mid-twenties, till life's end,
We tally the score, and comprehend.

So let's learn from our mistakes, and grow,
And face life's challenges, with courage and
show.
We'll rise from the ashes, stronger than before,
And find our way, forevermore.

Life's Canvas

We try to control everything, don't we?
Every little thing has to go our way.
But life's not a rulebook, it's more like a
rollercoaster.

We paint our world with a careful hand,
Each stroke precise, a perfect plan.
But life's a canvas, wild and free,
A masterpiece beyond our decree.

We're always comparing ourselves to others,
trying to look perfect online.
But real life is different.
It's about enjoying the ride, not just the photo
ops.

We chase perfection, a distant star,
Comparing lives, near and far.
Yet beauty blooms in nature's art,
Let's open hearts, a brand new start.

Life's a puzzle, we think we know,
Each piece in place, a perfect show.
But life's a river, wild and free,
Let's float along, happily.

Let's relax a bit, go with the flow, and see where
life takes us.

Let go of control, embrace the flow,
Where magic happens, softly grow.
In life's journey, let spirit soar,
Discover wonders, forevermore.

"LATE TWENTIES" CONNECTION AND PURPOSE

Communication: The Key to Connection

As adults, we often forget to speak,
Assuming thoughts will be clear and sleek.
But silence can breed confusion's art,
A heavy burden on every heart.

Sometimes we act, a bit too smart,
Ignoring others, a foolish start.
This silent treatment, a hurtful sting,
Can lead to problems, a painful thing.

If words are scarce, a childhood's plight,
Expressing feelings, a fading light.
Decisions become hard, a tangled maze,
A life of silence, a lonely phase.

So let's speak our minds, with clarity's grace,
Avoid confusion, a foolish chase.
Communication's key, a golden thread,
A bridge of understanding, well-bred.

The Rat Race of Twenties

In our twenties, we often run too fast,
Chasing money and things that don't last.
We compare ourselves to others all the time,
Feeling bad and sad, a heavy crime.

We forget to live our own lives, you see,
Always wanting what others have, can't be free.
This makes us feel down and lost, it's true,
Chasing dreams that are never new.

Depression can sneak up on you like a thief,
Making you feel lost and alone, a bitter grief.
You might feel restless and unhappy, a painful
plight,
Chasing shadows, without a light.

We should stop comparing and start to love,
Ourselves and others, from above.
Competition should be with ourselves, not others,
To find happiness within, yourself.

Beyond the Office Walls

Hey,

I go to the office daily, with an empty mind,
unsure of what to do.
I'm given daily tasks and told what to
accomplish.
I feel directionless in my life.
I've never truly defined what I want.
As days pass, I increasingly realize this isn't my
desired path.

Despite being conditioned to follow a specific
route – study, work, earn, marry – I yearn for
something different.

My heart races towards other interests,
making me question why I wasn't guided to take
a path I love.

Why am I here when my passion lies elsewhere?

Will I ever break free from this cage and pursue
what I truly love?
Will I ever be freed from this cage to fly far away
on the path where my soul and brain aligns in a
loving way?

Life's Three Stages: Childhood, Teenage and Adulthood

Childhood days, a carefree bliss,
Playing games, a joyful kiss.
Exploring the world, with wonder's gleam,
A magical time, a childhood dream.

Teenager years, a mix of fun and strife,
Discovering self, a second life.
Friendships formed, bonds so strong,
As we grew up, we belonged.

Adulthood's door, now wide and clear,
Responsibilities, a growing fear.
Yet, with each challenge, we learn and grow,
A journey of life, a steady flow.

From carefree days, to teenage strife,
To adulthood's challenges, a constant strife.
We've come so far, a journey's end,
A life well-lived, a faithful friend.

Gender Roles: A Changing Landscape

Men and women, worlds apart,
Different paths, a heavy heart.
He focuses on wealth, a constant race,
She balances life, a graceful grace.

He's unexpressive, a silent plea,
She's emotionally open, wild and free.
He struggles to meet, society's demand,
She fights for identity, a helping hand.

He battles the world, a warrior's plight,
She battles for equality, a shining light.
He's told to earn, a man's sole role,
She's told to care, a woman's goal.

But times are changing, a new dawn's hue,
She claims her space, a battle true.
For recognition, for her worth,
Not just for the household chores.

She's financially strong, a woman of might,
A force to be reckoned with, a shining light.
So let's break the mold, this outdated creed,
And celebrate equality, a noble deed.

A Man's Heart

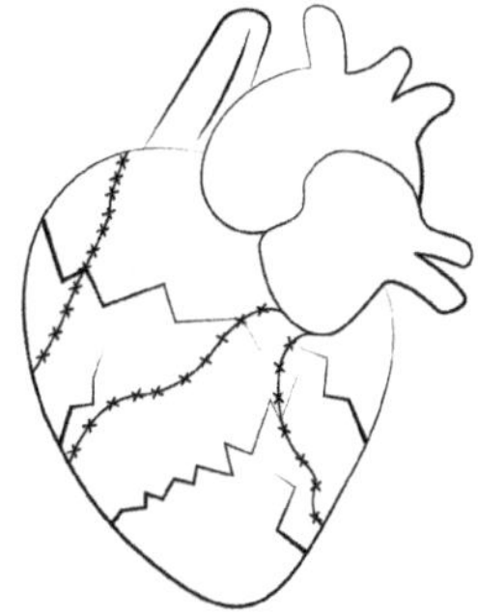

Behind the mask, a world untold,
A man's heart, brave and bold.
Often misunderstood, a silent plea,
A depth of feeling, wild and free.

He hides his pain, a stoic mask,
Afraid to show, a fragile task.
He carries burdens, heavy and deep,
A silent suffering, hard to keep.

But beneath the surface, a gentle soul,
A heart of gold, a loving goal.
He yearns for connection, a human touch,
A love that's true, beyond the much.

So let's see beyond the facade,
A man's heart, a treasure to applaud.
With understanding, let's break the mold,
And reveal the depths, a story untold.

A Woman's Heart

Like a garden, her heart grows and blooms,
Filled with emotions, vibrant hues.
A symphony of joy, sorrow, and strife,
A tapestry woven with threads of life.

A fortress of strength, yet tender and true,
A heart that beats, steady and new.
A universe within, vast and unknown,
A woman's heart, a treasure to be shown.

It yearns for connection, for love's sweet
embrace,
Yet fears rejection, vulnerability's place.
It dreams of equality, of freedom's flight,
Yet faces challenges, day and night.

A source of inspiration, a guiding light,
A woman's heart, a beautiful sight.
It's a world unto itself, a universe unknown,
A love to be cherished, a heart to be shown.

Love's Compass

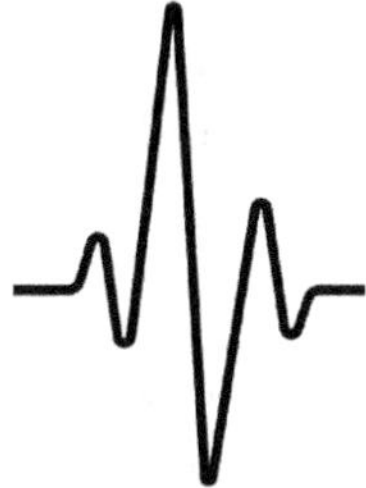

Is love an obstacle or a sanctuary?

Love is often seen as the greatest thing in the
world.
It can make people feel happy and excited.

But can it also change how we see our dreams
and goals?

A gentle hand or a forceful tide,
Does love uplift or does it hide?
For in its depths, can ambition reside,
Or is it a cage where dreams abide?

Why do people often abandon their previously
established goals upon finding love?

Dreams and goals, once a vibrant hue,
Can love's embrace dim their view?

I've observed individuals becoming lethargic
and unproductive for extended periods after
meeting their significant other.

Does love inherently weaken one's resolve,
or does it possess the power to strengthen and
redefine an individual?
Shouldn't love serve as a catalyst for personal
growth and development rather than a
hindrance?

It's like love is a strong current that can pull you
away from your path.
But love should also be a force that pushes you
forward, right?
It should inspire you to be a better person and
reach for your dreams.

Love should uplift, not define our end,
A partner in purpose, a steadfast friend.
Together we rise, stronger and more,
Love as our compass, forever to explore.

Food, Friends, and Fitness

Remember when eating was fun, no rules, just
pure joy?
Now, it's all about numbers and sizes.
Gyms and salads are the new cool,
but sometimes, we just crave a pizza or a
burger, right?

We act all high and mighty,
like we're better than everyone because we hit
the gym.
But let's be real, we miss hanging out with
friends, sharing food, and laughing without
guilt.
It's time to find a balance, enjoy life, and stop
being so hard on ourselves. After all, a little fun
won't hurt anyone.

Millennials, Gen Z, and Alphas: A Comparison

Millennials, Gen Z, and Alphas, a diverse blend,
Each generation, a unique friend.
Millennials, pioneers of the digital age,
Shaped by technology, a constant sage.

Gen Z, the next wave, a diverse crowd,
Socially conscious, fearless and proud.
Alphas, the youngest, a curious breed,
Digital natives, a future indeed.

In their twenties, they strive and dream,
Building careers, a shining gleam.
But work styles differ, a unique art,
Reflecting their values, from the very start.

Millennials, value work-life balance,
Seeking purpose, a constant trance.
Gen Z, prioritize social impact,
A cause-driven mindset, a powerful act.

Alphas, adaptable and creative minds,
Seeking flexibility, a new design.
Emotional intelligence, a common thread,
Empathy and understanding, well-bred.

IQs vary, a diverse range,
But intelligence comes in many forms, a change.
Each generation, a unique blend,
Shaping the future, a faithful friend.

Finding Your Calling - Paths to Passion

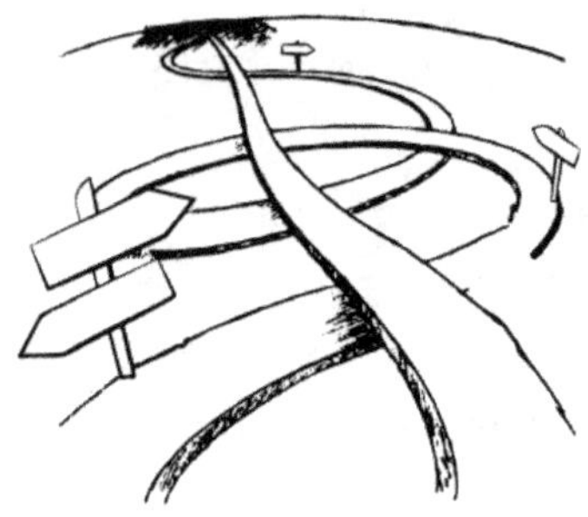

Some choose numbers, the world of CA,
A world of figures, precise and true,
Others circuits, engineers, that's their way,
Designing gadgets, that make our lives new.

MBA's plan, a business empire,
A world of deals, and corporate might,
PhDs delve deep, knowledge they acquire,
Pushing boundaries, reaching new heights.

Doctors heal, with a gentle touch,
A world of life, and hope renewed,
Scientists explore, seeking to touch,
The mysteries of the universe, pursued.

Entrepreneurs dream, building a brand,
A world of risk, and innovation's spark,
Artists express, their soul's command,
A world of color, and creativity's mark.

Each path unique, a different hue,
A colorful tapestry, woven with care,
No career greater, all have a view,
A world of purpose, beyond compare.
Choose wisely, a lifetime's call,
A second home, where passions fall,
Embrace your path, with heart and soul,
And let your journey unfold, whole.

Unheard Apologies

Words unspoken, feelings unspoken,
A heavy heart, forever broken.
We seek for closure, a peace of mind,
But apologies are hard to find.

We long to understand, to know we're not
wrong,
That we're not misunderstood, that something's
gone wrong.
A simple "sorry" can mend a broken heart,
Show us that we're not alone, torn apart.

Our actions and reactions, a tangled mess,
A path we never wanted, a painful distress.
Nights filled with tears, a mind that's lost and
confused,
Depression's weight, a world that's misused.

Fear and anxiety, a heavy load,
Taking us over, a desolate road.
But sometimes, we must let go, find peace within,
For some apologies, unheard and unseen.

Daughter's Delight

A riddle I pose, a question I ask,
Who is the one who'll always last?
A shining star, a guiding light,
A precious gift, a joy so bright.

She's always there, through thick and thin,
A constant source of love, within.
Who is she, this loving friend,
A daughter's love, without an end.

She will always bring abundance to you,
Even in her darkest times, it's true.
A daughter who will love you without any
prejudice,
Of getting worldly goods, she never wishes.

Instead, today's daughter will give you the same,
By being independent, financially sane.
She knows how to balance her life,
And love everyone around, without strife.

A Debt-ridden Dream

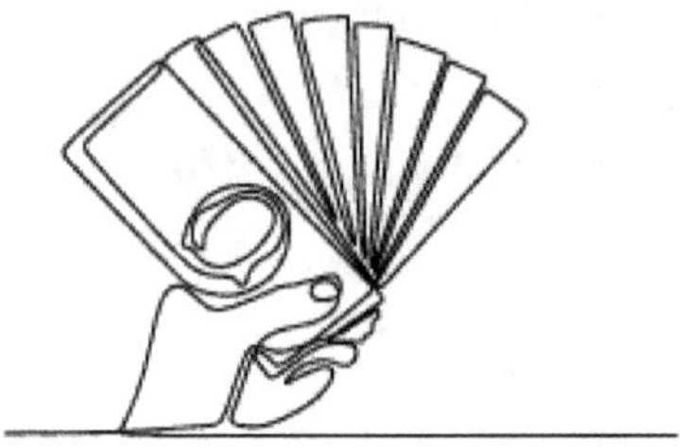

Once a dreamer, full of zest,
With aspirations, put to the test.
Loans grew, like weeds in the night,
Choking my dreams, dimming my light.

Income dwindled, savings were gone,
A prisoner of debt, a weary drone.
Each month a struggle, a constant fight,
To pay the dues, to keep the light.

No joy in possessions, no peace of mind,
Just the endless cycle, a burden unkind.
Debt crept in, a silent thief,
Stealing my future, leaving me bereft.

A chase for status, a foolish game,
A financial hole, a shameful shame.
No end in sight, a hopeless plight,
Trapped in the shadows, lost in the night.

So let this be a lesson learned,
A cautionary tale, a warning stern.
Before you chase the fleeting trend,
Think twice, and plan ahead.
For debt can be a heavy load,
A dangerous road.
Live within your means, be wise and bold,
And build a future, strong and gold.

The Human Puzzle - Karma's Cosmic Game

Is There a Greater Purpose?

In this vast universe, a cosmic stage,
A myriad of souls, from every age.
Some fight for identity, a place to stand,
While others yearn for respect, throughout the
land.

Desires of humans, a constant quest,
Some seek riches, wealth, put to the test.
Some crave the middle class, a steady pace,
While others embrace struggle, a life's embrace.

Some want to lead, above the rest,
While others lead, with hearts possessed.
Some give and give, with selfless grace,
But receivers often lack a grateful face.

People are diverse, their desires vary,
Some harm, some save, some fight, some marry.
Some use others, for their selfish gain,
While others share their skills, to ease the pain.

Some cheat, some stay loyal, a mixed array,
In this universe, where good and bad play.
Will karma balance all, with even hand,
To satisfy the needy, throughout the land?

Or is this chaos, a cosmic jest,
A never-ending test, put to the best?
Only time will tell, the final score,
As life unfolds, forevermore.

A Different Perspective

The world can feel so dark and gray,
A heavy weight, a dreary fray.
But change your view, a different sight,
A glimmer of hope, a guiding light.

Instead of dwelling on the wrong,
 Search for the good, where joy belongs.
In darkest times, find hope's bright gleam,
A flicker of light, a hopeful dream.

Explore new angles, a different view,
Discover depths you never knew.
A world transformed, a vibrant scene,
A fresh perspective, a life serene.

The Power of Words

Words, they're small, but mighty strong,
Can build or break, right or wrong.
A gentle touch, a healing balm,
Or a stinging dart, a hurtful calm.

In twenties, words can be a test,
A way to connect, or to confess.
They shape our thoughts, our minds and hearts,
Can mend or break, tear us apart.

So choose your words with careful art,
A gentle touch, a loving start.
For words can heal, can mend and mend,
A powerful tool, till life's end.

Healing Through Art

In life's relentless storm, we're often lost,
A weary soul, bearing life's heavy cost.
The world's a chaos, a swirling sea,
A heavy burden, weighing on me.

But art, a beacon, a guiding light,
Pierces through darkness, dispels the night.
A canvas blank, a soothing balm,
A way to express, to find our calm.

With every stroke, emotions flow,
A silent language, only we know.
Healing wounds, both old and new,
A sanctuary found, a spirit renewed.

Through music's melody, we find our peace,
A soothing balm, a sweet release.
The rhythm's beat, a steady guide,
Calming the soul, where worries abide.

In dance's grace, we find our strength,
A freedom of movement, a joyful length.
Our bodies express, what words can't say,
A healing journey, a brighter day.

Through words and stories, we share our pain,
Finding solace, a comforting rain.
A community of souls, a kindred tie,
A support system, to help us fly.

So let's embrace art, in all its forms,
A way to heal, to mend our storms.
A path to ourselves, a journey new,
A healing touch, forever true.

The Pressure to Settle Down

Twenty-something, a time to roam,
To find your path, to make your home.
But whispers creep, a constant sound,
"Settle down now, don't be bound."

Society's gaze, a watchful eye,
A ticking clock, a reason why.
To find a love, a steady hand,
A house, a job, a life well-planned.

But hearts may yearn for something more,
To explore the world, to unlock the door.
To chase dreams, to reach for the sky,
Before the clock ticks time goodbye.

So let your spirit soar and fly,
Don't let the pressure make you cry.
For life is short, and time is fleet,
So follow your heart, and make it sweet.

You Are Number One

You're special, one of a kind, that's true,
So value yourself, me and you!
Do things for others, that's great,
But don't forget yourself, no wait!

Don't need their cheers, don't need their praise,
Shine bright, in your own amazing ways.
Be kind and helpful, that's the plan,
But number one, you always can.

So stand tall, head held high,
You're a superstar, reach for the sky!
Don't let others dim your light,
You're awesome, shining oh so bright!

Reconnection

I've chased the world, forgot my heart,
Ignored your whispers, torn apart.
You're my compass, my guiding light,
Please come back, make everything right.

I'm lost without you, it's plain to see,
Let's reunite, wild and free.
I promise to listen, to care and share,
Let's build our bond, beyond compare.

Calling My Soul Home

Lost in the echoes of my own desire,
Ignoring your whispers, a fading fire.
You watch from a distance, a silent plea,
To reconnect, set my spirit free.

I've chased shadows, a fruitless art,
Neglecting the garden of my heart.
Fear has crept in, a chilling cold,
As our bond weakens, the story untold.

I yearn for your warmth, your guiding light,
To fill my world with hope and might.
Let's reconcile, make a fresh start,
You and I, together, heart to heart.